The Book Journey Mentor's™ Guide to Self-Publishing

The Workbook

Conscious Dreams
PUBLISHING

The Book Journey Mentor's™ Guide to Self-Publishing: Workbook

Daniella Blechner.

Non Fiction Publishing Workbook

Copyright © 2016 by Daniella Blechner

All rights reserved. This book or any portion thereof may not be reproduced, shared publicly or privately or used in any manner whatsoever without the express written permission of the publisher except for the use of brief quotations in a book review.

Printed in the United Kingdom

First Printing 2016 Conscious Dreams Publishing.

www.consciousdreamspublishing.com

ISBN: 978-1913674212

Conscious Dreams
PUBLISHING

This book belongs to

....

Contents

1. Getting to the Heart of Me 1
2. Ingramspark and ISBNs: Publishing and Distribution 41
3. Editing: The Big Cut 45
4. Typesetting and Layout 47
5. Cover Design 51
6. Promotion 53
7. How to Get Your Book in the Press 61
8. Securing Retailers 63

WHO IS MY BOOK JOURNEY MENTOR™?

Hello, my name is Daniella, founder of Conscious Dreams Publishing, and I will also be your Book Journey Mentor™. I am passionate about empowering you through the self-publishing process and assisting you in fulfilling your vision.

Publishing a book is not so much about the physical process of publishing but the journey you have planned for your book's life. Almost anyone can publish a book, however my mission and vision is to coach and publish authors with stories and books that uplift, motivate, encourage and inspire and ensure that your book is of the high quality you deserve. I established **Conscious Dreams Publishing,** with a clear vision and purpose and I am excited about assisting you with setting up your own publishing brand and delivering your book. Your book is too valuable to go unread!

In 2014, I achieved one of my biggest achievements to date (after climbing Kilimanjaro and getting to the top with the flu!!) and published my debut book *Mr Wrong*. *Mr Wrong* hit three bestseller Lists rising above *The Joy of Sex*, *Women Love Bitches* and the infamous Steve Harvey's *Think Like a Man, Act Like a Lady* within hours of being published. I can share with you strategies that boost your chances of getting that sought after bestseller status too! I have since gone on to publish seven other books of my own, 200 authors' books and mentored nearly 300 aspiring authors.

Writing and publishing a book is a dream many people share but with conscious effort, commitment and the right assistance, this dream can finally become a reality.

- www.consciousdreamspublishing.com
- www.consciousdreamsbookshop.com
- daniella@consciousdreamspublishing.com
- www.facebook.com/consciousdreamspublishing
- www.instagram.com/consciousdreamspublishing
- www.linkedin.com/in/daniellablechner

"Be the author of your own destiny."

Daniella ☺

1. Getting to the Heart of Me

I was motivated to take the first step with Daniella, The Book Journey Mentor™, because

....
....
....
....
....
....
....
....
....
....
....
....
....

I want my story to have impact because ....

....

....

....

....

....

....

....

....

....

I will create my legacy by ....

....

....

....

....

....

....

....

....

....

Reinforcing Your Motivation

Whenever or, if ever, you are in doubt or feel overwhelmed by the process, always revisit these three questions. There is a lot to learn during the self-publishing process. Not only are you birthing a book but you are responsible for its entire journey including the marketing and promotion of your book. Yes, there are marketing and PR companies you can employ to relieve some of this, however ultimately the life of the book is determined by the passion, motivation and belief instilled in the author.

What kept me going, and still keeps me going, is my absolute clarity about why I am doing what I am doing, what motivated me and what legacy I want to leave. We may not always know what we are doing, but we must certainly know why we are doing what we do. Hold this "why" in your spirit so firmly that in every interview you give, every article you write and every talk you give, it shines through with absolute clarity.

Why did I write *Mr Wrong*? I wrote *Mr Wrong* because I wanted to unite, inspire and empower women through providing them with a platform to tell and share their stories. I wanted to provide a safe space where women could examine, question and challenge limiting belief systems they may have about love, relationships, and most importantly, themselves. I wanted to break down the barriers we often have about admitting our failures in relationships and embrace them, allowing us, together, to go on a journey of self-discovery as all relationships start with Self.

I am passionate about giving voice to others and empowering others by helping them discover their true value and worth. This is the legacy I envisioned from the beginning. Through the publishing process, you too can create legacies of significance that positively impact the world for generations to come. I believe your knowledge and experiences are powerful and must be utilised for a greater purpose.

Remembering why we do things and who we want to impact helps to ground us and keeps us focused. It also allows us to refine our vision. We may be offered interviews, be asked to endorse events and products or collaborate with others, and we must be sure that they are in alignment with what we stand for and are motivated by. Not every opportunity presented to you will be in your best interest, and knowing who we truly are, what we believe in and what we want to represent will help you create a laser focus. You will automatically start to attract opportunities that will benefit you and your mission.

WHO AM I SURROUNDED BY?

Write a list of the top five people you regularly spend time with.

1. ....
2. ....
3. ....
4. ....
5. ....

The people above are in your closest circle. Read the following statements; now write down how you think they are most likely to respond. Remember, the thoughts and words of those in your inner circle become the subconscious thoughts you begin to grow. If the people in your inner circle drag you down, you can choose to continue to allow them to, eliminate them or limit the time you spend with them. I strongly advise you increase the amount of time you spend with those who have a positive influence on you, those who support you and those you can learn and grow from.

1. I am writing a book. What do you think?

2. I want to become a best-selling author.

3. I want to inspire and empower others through my writing.

4. I have a purpose to my life and want to fulfil it. Will you help me?

5. Will you support me with my book launch?

PERSON 1

Response to:

1. I am writing a book. What do you think?

   ....
   ....
   ....

2. I want to become a best-selling author.

   ....
   ....
   ....

3. I want to inspire and empower others through my writing.

   ....
   ....
   ....

4. I have a purpose to my life and want to fulfil it. Will you help me?

   ....
   ....
   ....

5. Will you support me with my book launch?

   ....
   ....
   ....

PERSON 2

Response to:

1. I am writing a book. What do you think?

   ....
   ....
   ....

2. I want to become a best-selling author.

   ....
   ....
   ....

3. I want to inspire and empower others through my writing.

   ....
   ....
   ....

4. I have a purpose to my life and want to fulfil it. Will you help me?

   ....
   ....
   ....

5. Will you support me with my book launch?

   ....
   ....
   ....

PERSON 3

Response to:

1. I am writing a book. What do you think?

   ....
   ....
   ....

2. I want to become a best-selling author.

   ....
   ....
   ....

3. I want to inspire and empower others through my writing.

   ....
   ....
   ....

4. I have a purpose to my life and want to fulfil it. Will you help me?

   ....
   ....
   ....

5. Will you support me with my book launch?

   ....
   ....
   ....

PERSON 4

Response to:

1. **I am writing a book. What do you think?**

   ....
   ....
   ....

2. **I want to become a best-selling author.**

   ....
   ....
   ....

3. **I want to inspire and empower others through my writing.**

   ....
   ....
   ....

4. **I have a purpose to my life and want to fulfil it. Will you help me?**

   ....
   ....
   ....

5. **Will you support me with my book launch?**

   ....
   ....
   ....

PERSON 5

Response to:

1. I am writing a book. What do you think?

   ....
   ....
   ....

2. I want to become a best-selling author.

   ....
   ....
   ....

3. I want to inspire and empower others through my writing.

   ....
   ....
   ....

4. I have a purpose to my life and want to fulfil it. Will you help me?

   ....
   ....
   ....

5. Will you support me with my book launch?

   ....
   ....
   ....

SUCCESS VS FAILURE

Which success story inspired you most and why?

....
....
....
....
....
....
....
....

Which author inspires you most and why?

....
....
....
....
....
....
....
....

Complete this statement:

Success is ....

SUCCESS AND THE SUBCONSCIOUS MIND

Writing and publishing a book is an enormous feat and an exciting journey. I want this journey to be as positive as possible for you. So first, before anything, we must work on your mindset.

We are multi-dimensional beings made up of mind, body, soul, and spirit. The mind is divided into the conscious, subconscious and the unconscious. Most of the time, we live in our minds; we are either thinking about the past or worrying about the future. Very rarely do we live in the present. All of our thoughts and experiences are downloaded to our subconscious mind on a daily basis. Hour by hour, minute by minute, second by second. But first, what is the difference between our conscious and subconscious mind?

Our mind can be compared to an iceberg. Everything we see at the top (the tip) is our conscious mind. Everything that resides below and hidden is our subconscious mind. Are we programming our minds for success or failure?

Conscious Mind

According the Cambridge Dictionary, there are two definitions of consciousness:

1. **consciousness** *noun* [U] (UNDERSTANDING) the state of understanding and realizing something

2. **consciousness** *noun* [U] (AWAKE) the state of being awake, thinking, and knowing what is happening around you

The conscious mind is everything that resides inside our awareness. This includes perceptions, sensations, feelings, beliefs, likes, and dislikes. It has an innate ability to rationalise, analyse and process information, and it allows us to make decisions based on logic. The conscious mind only makes up 10% of our minds. It is the tip of the iceberg so to speak.

Conscious Dreams Publishing

I chose to name my publishing company Conscious Dreams Publishing as I believe in the power of the conscious mind. I believe that when we make declarations and conscious decisions we are more intentional. We are building our empires and dreams based on a strong desire and intention to succeed in fulfilling our dreams based on a conscious decision to create thoughts, words and actions that fall into alignment with those dreams. Lots of us say we want to do things and talk eloquently of our dreams but lack the conscious effort and awareness to do everything possible to bring them into our realm. I don't believe dreams should exist only in a fantasy land of hope, but that we must do everything possible to manifest them into our conscious world. Our conscious mind is powerful when we wish to create all that we desire.

What conscious thoughts can you chose to create?

....

....

....

....

....

....

When was the last time you created a positive thought about your book?

....

....

....

....

....

....

Subconscious Mind

The subconscious mind is like a memory bank. Every thought, every word, every action and every experience is stored in the subconscious mind. Permanently. According to Brian Tracy[1], author of *Change Your Thinking Change Your Life*, by the time you are 21, you would have stored 100 times the information stored in the British Encyclopaedia. You may be surprised to learn that it makes up to 90% of your mind!

Think of your mind as a computer. Your subconscious mind is like its loyal servant. It is purely subjective, does not differentiate between "positive" or "negative" and has no ability to reason, make decisions or make choices that are good for you. It simply downloads the information you tell it and its function is to make sure your patterns, behaviour and habits respond exactly to the thoughts, words, actions and experiences you feed it. Our subconscious mind is a powerful tool. It can retrieve any given experience, thought, chapter or verse once accessed. It is far more reliable than our conscious memory and it is for this reason we must seek to truly understand the power of our conscious mind.

We must be aware of our thoughts at all times. Is what we are thinking progressing us forward, encouraging us to be the best that we can be, to try new things without fear or are we simply reacting to world outside us and remaining in our comfort zones? According to Brian Tracy, *"Your subconscious mind causes you to feel emotionally and physically uncomfortable whenever you attempt to do anything new or different, or to change any of your established patterns of behaviour."*

How do you react when things feel uncomfortable?

....
....
....

When was the last time you stepped out of your comfort zone?

....
....
....

---

1   http://www.briantracy.com/blog/general/understanding-your-subconscious-mind/

THOUGHT JOURNAL

Day 1: _____

For 7 Days pay attention to your thoughts. Write down the Top 7 recurring thoughts.

1. ....

2. ....

3. ....

4. ....

5. ....

6. ....

7. ....

"Your worst enemy cannot harm you as much as your own unguarded thoughts."

Buddha

Now ask yourself these questions.

- Are these thoughts serving me at all?

- How did these thoughts make me feel?

- Do I want more of this feeling?

- How are these thoughts manifesting things that occur in my life?

- How can you create better (even better) feel-good thoughts?

- Is it the thoughts that are creating circumstances or are my thoughts simply a reaction to my circumstances?

THOUGHT JOURNAL

Day 2: _____

For 7 Days pay attention to your thoughts. Write down the Top 7 recurring thoughts.

1. ....
....
....

2. ....
....
....

3. ....
....
....

4. ....
....
....

5. ....
....
....

6. ....
....
....

7. ....
....
....

Now ask yourself these questions.

- Are these thoughts serving me at all?

- How did these thoughts make me feel?

- Do I want more of this feeling?

- How are these thoughts manifesting things that occur in my life?

- How can you create better (even better) feel-good thoughts?

- Is it the thoughts that are creating circumstances or are my thoughts simply a reaction to my circumstances?

THOUGHT JOURNAL

Day 3: _____

For 7 Days pay attention to your thoughts. Write down the Top 7 recurring thoughts.

1. ....
   ....
   ....

2. ....
   ....
   ....

3. ....
   ....
   ....

4. ....
   ....
   ....

5. ....
   ....
   ....

6. ....
   ....
   ....

7. ....
   ....
   ....

Now ask yourself these questions.

- Are these thoughts serving me at all?

- How did these thoughts make me feel?

- Do I want more of this feeling?

- How are these thoughts manifesting things that occur in my life?

- How can you create better (even better) feel-good thoughts?

- Is it the thoughts that are creating circumstances or are my thoughts simply a reaction to my circumstances?

THOUGHT JOURNAL

Day 4: _____

For 7 Days pay attention to your thoughts. Write down the Top 7 recurring thoughts.

1. ....
   ....
   ....

2. ....
   ....
   ....

3. ....
   ....
   ....

4. ....
   ....
   ....

5. ....
   ....
   ....

6. ....
   ....
   ....

7. ....
   ....
   ....

Now ask yourself these questions.

- Are these thoughts serving me at all?

- How did these thoughts make me feel?

- Do I want more of this feeling?

- How are these thoughts manifesting things that occur in my life?

- How can you create better (even better) feel-good thoughts?

- Is it the thoughts that are creating circumstances or are my thoughts simply a reaction to my circumstances?

THOUGHT JOURNAL

Day 5: _____

For 7 Days pay attention to your thoughts. Write down the Top 7 recurring thoughts.

1. ....
   ....
   ....

2. ....
   ....
   ....

3. ....
   ....
   ....

4. ....
   ....
   ....

5. ....
   ....
   ....

6. ....
   ....
   ....

7. ....
   ....
   ....

1. Getting to the Heart of Me

Now ask yourself these questions.

- Are these thoughts serving me at all?

- How did these thoughts make me feel?

- Do I want more of this feeling?

- How are these thoughts manifesting things that occur in my life?

- How can you create better (even better) feel-good thoughts?

- Is it the thoughts that are creating circumstances or are my thoughts simply a reaction to my circumstances?

THOUGHT JOURNAL

Day 6: _____

For 7 Days pay attention to your thoughts. Write down the Top 7 recurring thoughts.

1. ....
   ....
   ....

2. ....
   ....
   ....

3. ....
   ....
   ....

4. ....
   ....
   ....

5. ....
   ....
   ....

6. ....
   ....
   ....

7. ....
   ....
   ....

Now ask yourself these questions.

- Are these thoughts serving me at all?

- How did these thoughts make me feel?

- Do I want more of this feeling?

- How are these thoughts manifesting things that occur in my life?

- How can you create better (even better) feel-good thoughts?

- Is it the thoughts that are creating circumstances or are my thoughts simply a reaction to my circumstances?

THOUGHT JOURNAL

Day 7: _____

For 7 Days pay attention to your thoughts. Write down the Top 7 recurring thoughts.

1. ....
   ....
   ....

2. ....
   ....
   ....

3. ....
   ....
   ....

4. ....
   ....
   ....

5. ....
   ....
   ....

6. ....
   ....
   ....

7. ....
   ....
   ....

Now ask yourself these questions.

- Are these thoughts serving me at all?

- How did these thoughts make me feel?

- Do I want more of this feeling?

- How are these thoughts manifesting things that occur in my life?

- How can you create better (even better) feel-good thoughts?

- Is it the thoughts that are creating circumstances or are my thoughts simply a reaction to my circumstances?

CREATING INTENTIONS

Intentions are something I speak and work with a lot in both my personal life and the workshops I run. They are mentioned in *Mr Wrong* to aid women attracting the right partners and relationships that they want in their lives. We also work on setting intentions that are in alignment with our vision for any area of our lives in my workshop *7 Steps to Creating the Greatest Version of You*.

Intentions are crucial if we choose to walk in our purpose and live the Life we want.

Extract from *Mr Wrong* Chapter 9: Start With You

Setting Your Intentions

"An intention is a higher consciousness thought. It is a desire expressed with absolute faith that the outcome will transpire. An intention is an expectation simply handed over to the Universe in order for it to be fulfilled—a bit like placing an order at a restaurant and then waiting for the meal to arrive. When we place the order or express the intention, we expect the meal to arrive. We don't hound and harass or follow the waiter into the kitchen to ensure they have placed the order correctly or get into the kitchen and start cooking it ourselves. We have faith that the order will arrive. Just as we say thank you when we place our order and again when our order arrives, we must do the same with our intentions. Gratitude plays a major role in intention setting."

What Intentions do you have for your book?

Created by Photoangel — Freepik.com

Post It Note Exercise

No one fully understands the powerful potential of the human brain, but the fact is that your brain doesn't know the difference between a real experience and a virtual one. The experience is not really happening, but your mind expects it to happen because that is the reality you've created for it. When it does happen, the expectation is reinforced.

In the same way, you can literally think your way to any new experience you intend, for example, being a Bestselling Author or signing books at your sell out book launch. Your brain will see this as a real experience and expect this experience to take place.

So, let's get manifesting!

Using the Post-Its on the next page, write down your intentions. Make sure you use the "I am" or "I have" form. Using the present tense causes the subconscious to believe the intent has already manifested, that it actually happened and was a real experience. These thought patterns attract energy that resonates on the same vibration as like attracts like.

Your intentions must be clear and specific. It's not enough to simply say "I want a good book". Think about the impact you want to have on your readers. How do you want them to feel? If you want to inspire and empower others, try this: "My book XXXX will inspire and empower (enter audience here) all over the world."

Read your intentions aloud. You can read them once, twice three times or even sing them. How you choose to read them is up to you. As you read them, try to imagine how it feels to have this manifested.

EXERCISE

Visualise it actually happening. (Note down what you see)

....
....
....
....

If you are sensitive to energy, note down how reading each intention affects your energy.

....
....
....
....

What sensations are you experiencing?

....
....
....
....

Do you feel them in your physical energy or as emotional energy?

....
....
....
....

MY INTENTIONS

SUCCESS vs SIGNIFICANCE

Now that we have evaluated who we have in our inner circle and understand the power of success and our subconscious mind, let's differentiate between success and significance.

I want you to watch this inspirational short video of Nido Qubein. Nido Qubein came to the United States as a teenager with no knowledge of English, no contacts and only $50 in his pocket. Today he is a successful businessman and award-winning motivational speaker. Watch, take notes and evaluate how you can create an impactful book of significance.

https://www.youtube.com/watch?v=0MZfWw27jTA

"Success by any measure is secular; significance by any measure is spiritual."

Nido Qubein

Notes on Nido Qubein

How have I created a book of significance?

....

....

....

....

How will my book positively impact others?

....

....

....

....

MY SUCCESS MANTRA

I am open to receiving success

Success flows abundantly in my life

I attract success and positive opportunities to me

I AM success

Now write 4 more of your own.

....

....

....

....

WHY PUBLISH?

List 3 reasons you want to publish your book.

1. ....
   ....
   ....
   ....
   ....
   ....

2. ....
   ....
   ....
   ....
   ....
   ....

3. ....
   ....
   ....
   ....
   ....
   ....

WHAT HOLDS YOU BACK?

Now that you have three strong reasons as to why you want to publish, write down three things that may have held you back in the past. The reason for doing this exercise is because I want you to be easily able to identify when these so-called obstacles begin to show up. Today, you are going to create a strategy so that you are ready for them if they try to show up on your book journey. There is a strategy for everything that seems to hold us back in life, and if there isn't one, your subconscious is going to create one.

What holds me back	Strategies
Self-belief	• Use some of the success intentions/mantras • Create some intentions around self-belief • Visualise yourself being successful and achieving your vision • Record your negative thought processes on a pad. Now change the negative thoughts to positive statements. Record these statements via audio and listen to these positive statements • Ensure you are surrounding yourself with positive people who believe in you

1. Getting to the Heart of Me

What holds me back	Strategies

What holds me back	Strategies

2. IngramSpark and ISBNs: Publishing and Distribution

ISBNs

What does ISBN stand for?

....

....

What is an ISBN and why is it important?

....

....

How many ISBNs do you need per book?

....

How many formats of your book will you have? Specify EPUB / mobi / PDF / paper back / hard back[2]?

....

....

---

[2] Make sure all this information from this question onwards is included on your Nielson's application form.

Will your book be paper back or hard back?

....

What is the name of your publishing brand?

....

What is the name of your distributing company?

....

What trim size have you chosen?

....

Record your ISBNs, book title and format here:

ISBN Number	Title	Format

IngramSpark Book Template

All Conscious Dreams mentees are required to purchase ISBNs before they begin the coaching programme if they want to publish under their own publishing brand. Your ISBN will be printed on the back of the book together with the barcode. This will be generated by IngramSpark when you use their template cover generator. See template example below for a standard 6" x 9" book (Standard US Trade size)

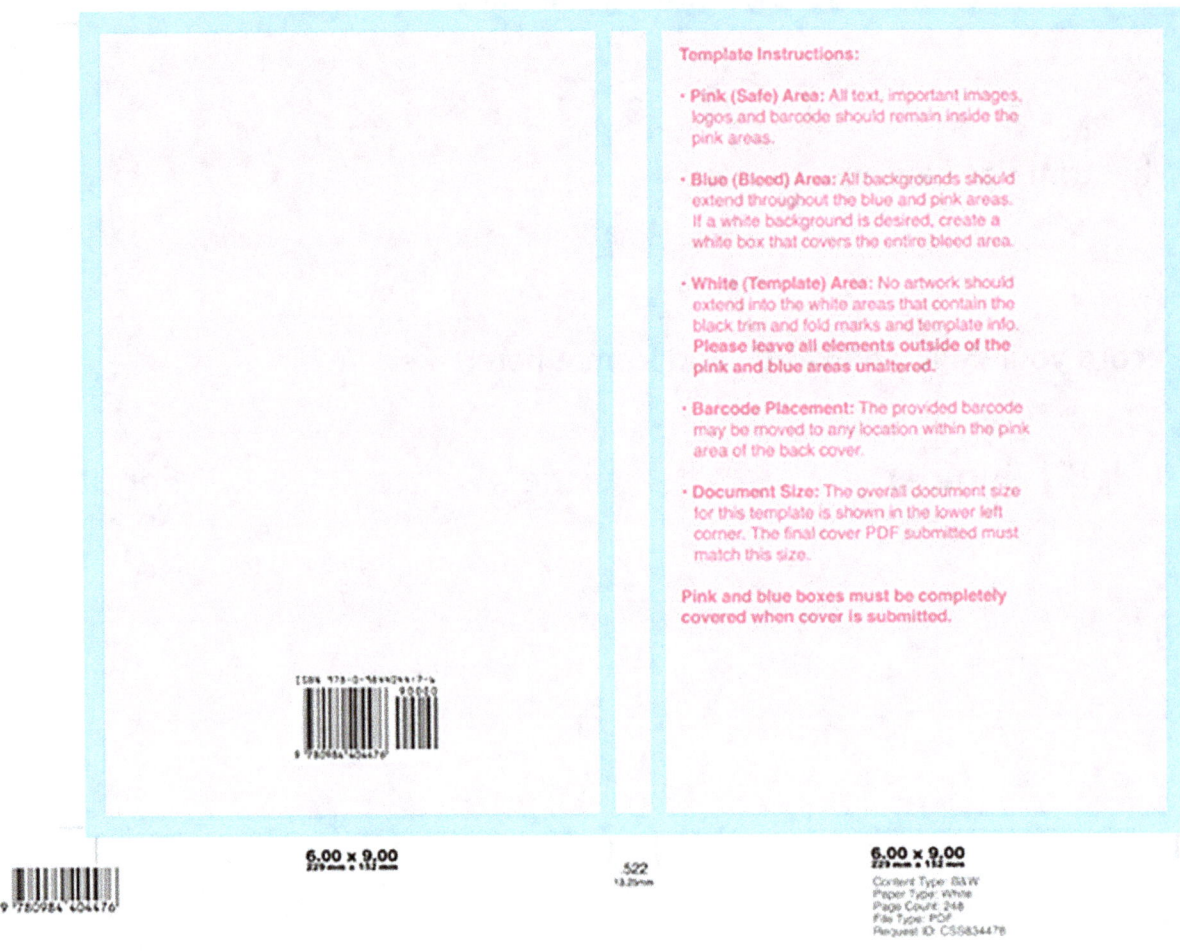

Your Happy Child Book Full Cover Example

44 The Book Journey Mentor's Guide to Self-Publishing: The Workbook | Daniella Blechner

3. Editing: The Big Cut

Three different types of editing are:

1. ....

   What does that mean?

   ....

   ....

2. ....

   What does that mean?

   ....

   ....

3. ....

   What does that mean?

   ....

   ....

Have a look at your manuscript. Which type of editing do you think you need most assistance with?

THE BLURB

Write your 200 word blurb here. Remember to make it:
- **Punchy**
- **Intriguing**
- **Articulate**
- **Clear**
- **Informative**

My Blurb for ....

....

....

....

....

....

....

....

....

....

....

....

....

....

4. Typesetting and Layout

Your Title Verso

{ENTER NAME OF BOOK and YOUR NAME}

{ENTER TYPE OF BOOK}

Copyright © {YEAR OF PUBLISH and NAME OF AUTHOR}

All rights reserved. This book or any portion thereof may not be reproduced or used in any manner whatsoever without the express written permission of the publisher except for the use of brief quotations in a book review.

Printed in the United Kingdom

First Printing {YEAR OF PUBLISH, PUBLISHING COMPANY, YOURNAME}

ISBN: {YOUR ISBN NUMBER}

OPTIONAL: WEBSITE ADDRESSES

YOUR BOOK'S BONES

Let's work out the sequence of your book. Structure is important. Use the Book Journey Mentor™ Guide to refer to each section of a book. Make a list of those you would like to include. Remember you do not need to include all sections, infact most books do not, just the sections that are relevant to you. Jot down the list of sections and feel free to add notes about what you may include in each section.

1. ....
   ....
   ....

2. ....
   ....
   ....

3. ....
   ....
   ....

4. ....
   ....
   ....

5. ....
   ....
   ....

6. ....
   ....
   ....

7. ....
....

8. ....
....
....

9. ....
....
....

10. ....
....
....

Other notes....

....
....
....
....
....
....
....
....

48

5. Cover Design

Brainstorm your ideas for your book cover

1. Title:
   ....

2. Subtitle/Shoutline/Tagline:
   ....
   ....

3. Image:
   ....
   ....

4. Colour Scheme:
   ....

5. Author Name:
   ....

6. Reviews:
   ....
   ....

7. Awards:
   ....
   ....

Have a go at sketching your book cover here...

6. Promotion

My strategies to promote my book

1. ....

   How?

   ....
   ....
   ....
   ....
   ....
   ....

2. ....

   How?

   ....
   ....
   ....
   ....
   ....
   ....

3. ....

   How?

   ....
   ....
   ....
   ....
   ....
   ....

4. ....

   How?

   ....
   ....
   ....
   ....
   ....

5. ....

   How?

   ....
   ....
   ....

6. ....

....
....
....
....

6. ....

How?

....
....
....
....
....
....

7. ....

How?

....
....
....
....
....
....
....

MY BOOK LAUNCH

Close your eyes and visualise that day. How would you describe the atmosphere? What colours can you see? What energy are you bringing to the book launch? What do the attendee's facial expressions look like? This day will come and you will want to enjoy every second of it.

It is important to plan for the event and this means having a very clear vision for the evening.

Draw an image of what you visualise.

Make notes on the following:

1. **What sort of book launch do you want to have?**

   (A reading, author talk, networking, debate?)

   ....

2. **What sort of venue do you want to use?**

   (Library, cafe, bookstore, bar, community hall, restaurant)

   ....

3. **What is your budget?**

   (Account for everything before you book anything)

   ....

4. **What extra added value are you offering your guests?**

   (Catering, goodie bags, special offers)

   ....

5. **What special offers are you promoting on the day?**

   (50% off 2nd book, merchandise, KINDLE PROMOTION ON DAY OF PUBLISH (See Bestseller doc)

   ....

   ....

6. **How can you stay in contact with your guests?**

   (Mailing list, card jar?)

   ....

7. **Make a list of things you need on the day.**

   (Photographer, videographer, clipboard, projector, chairs)

   ....

   ....

6. Promotion

Planning My Book Launch

I have great respect for an organisation known as 100 Black Men Of London[3], a community based charity led by Black men, who deliver programmes and activities focused on Mentoring, Education, Economic Empowerment and Leadership. Their events are always flawlessly run and this is due to excellent planning and implementation. They have kindly allowed me to share with you the Event Schedule they use to plan their events. You are able to use this tool for your own book launch.

SCHEDULE – CHECKLIST

1. **Define the event clearly in no more than 15 words**

EVENT TITLE	DESCRIPTION (IN 15 WORDS)

2. **Assemble the Team and choose**

PROJECT LEADER	
DEPUTY PROJECT LEADER	
TEAM MEMBERS (Has each team member been delegated a specific area of responsibility i.e. marketing, sponsorship, dealings with suppliers etc.?)	

---

3 http://www.100bml.org/ *Special Thanks to 100 Black Men of London*

3. **What are the aims and objectives of the event?**

OBJECTIVES FOR THE BOOK LAUNCH (Do these objectives tie in with our Strategic Objectives and core focus)	
OBJECTIVES FOR OTHERS (Who is the target audience for the event and how will they benefit?)	

4. **Details of the Event**

DATE	
LOCATION/VENUE	
TIME OF THE EVENT	
USERS (who is expected to attend?)	
NUMBERS EXPECTED & CAPACITY OF VENUE	

PRODUCTS & SERVICES (all the products and services or activities will be present at the event? i.e. food, drink, bouncy castle etc.)	
EVENT TIME PLAN (time plan for the day itself)	
RESOURCES & MATERIALS NEEDED FOR THE DAY (mailing lists, donations box, feedback forms, camera, video, AV equipment, registration list & computer, petty cash etc.)	
MANPOWER RESOURCES NEEDED FOR THE DAY (helpers, registration, security, cameraman, videographer, stewards etc.)	
BOOKING PROCESS FOR THE EVENT (how will people book for the event)	
ENTRY REQUIREMENTS	

7. How to Get Your Book in the Press

Getting in the press can be tough but it is all about your tenacity, innovation and passion. You may end up contacting so many journalists that you forget who you have contacted and who you may need to follow up on.

My advice to you is to make a list of media you wish to contact with a brief explanation as to why. It might be an idea to create an excel spreadsheet with the contact details and websites of each magazine. When you contact them, record the date and time as well as any follow up phone calls or emails you have made. This way you have created an easy tool that will help you measure and track the progress of your quest to get in the press.

Magazines

1. ....
2. ....
3. ....
4. ....
5. ....
6. ....
7. ....

Radio stations

1. ....
2. ....
3. ....
4. ....
5. ....
6. ....
7. ....

Bloggers

1. ....
2. ....
3. ....
4. ....
5. ....
6. ....
7. ....

TV Programmes

1. ....
2. ....
3. ....
4. ....
5. ....
6. ....
7. ....

8. Securing Retailers

Make a list of potential reviewers you will approach

1. ....
2. ....
3. ....
4. ....
5. ....
6. ....
7. ....
8. ....
9. ....
10. ....

ADVANCED INFORMATION SHEET

Title: Mr Wrong

Author: Daniella Blechner

Keywords: Dating, relationships, love

BIC CODE: VFVG

Size: 6 x 9

Page Extent: 296

Publication Date: 20th September 2014

Format: Paperback

ISBN: 9780992991906

Price: £12.99

Language: English

Publisher: Conscious Dreams Publishing
www.consciousdreamspublishing.com

Blog: www.dingdongitsmrwrong.com

Contact: daniella'consciousdreamspublishing.com

Selling Points:

- Sneak peeks into real life relationship stories and witty dating disasters
- A Mr Wrong manual!
- Exercises, quizzes, questionnaires designed to engage the reader interactively and self-discover
- A balance of humour, poignancy and self-exploration
- Men have their say too!
- No preaching, teaching or rules!

Summary

Do you ever feel as though you will never meet the right man? Are your relationships leaving you wondering what you're doing wrong? Do you attract the same type of man, repeating the same negative patterns over and over again? If you find yourself thinking 'Here we go again' or 'I've been here before', if you're dating men who love you and leave you emotionally wounded and insecure, or if you're wondering why you just can't seem to get it right, I have news for you. You are simply dating the wrong men.

Mr. Wrong is an insightful and witty exploration as to why some women continually attract the wrong men. This powerful collection of humorous, insightful, and entertaining stories are written by women from across the world that have encountered and overcome toxic Mr. Wrong relationships.

The book is designed to unite, inspire, and empower women through interactive quizzes, exercises, and meditations. Through them, you can explore, question, and challenge negative belief systems that are attracting damaging connections. It enables a positive journey of self-discovery that breaks the cycle of defeating relationships and ultimately leads to a healthy outcome. Mr. Wrong gives women the courage to turn their pain into Power and their adversities into Opportunities. It also gives space for celebrating Mr. Right by acknowledging men's valuable relationship stories too. Do men get a bad rap? What role do women play in creating Mr. Wrong?

About the Author

Daniella Blechner is a South London based writer whose professional writing journey began by writing comedy sketches for Youth Project *Phenomenon '98* featuring Gina Yashere and Richard Blackwood.

She produced and wrote her first short film *Connexions*, which was Nominated for Best Screenplay at the BFM Short Film Awards in 2006 and won "Best Open Deck film" when screened at the Cutting East Festival and won the 2007 Film Fund Award from Lewisham Film Initiative to complete her poetry based short drama *Hair We Are* for the Black History Month Short Film Challenge. *Hair We Are* won the 3rd Best Film at the Images of Black Women Film Festival and has been screened at Chicago International Children's Film Festival, Pan African Film Festival, LA and BAMKids Film Festival in New York and was also screened on The Community Channel and www.itvlocal.com. Shortly afterwards, Daniella was shortlisted as a writer for Channel 4's Coming Up initiative having written a short film idea about love, marriage and dysfunctional families.

After a decade of dating disasters, Daniella chose to claim her story to empower others and wrote her debut book Mr Wrong, "a humorous and insightful exploration into why some women continually attract Mr Wrong and how to set out on a path to Mr Right."

Sketch your own Advanced Information Sheet.

8. Securing into Retailers

YOUR BOOK, YOUR JOURNEY

We have come to the end of the road, but remember you are in control of your book's journey at all times. You are more than equipped to continue along the path of self-publishing. Publishing the book is the easy part, now it's time to promote, market and nurture your book. If I was to say one thing to you, it would be:

> *"Remember who you are, remember your story and how you want to impact your reader."*

This is the key to everything. I've enjoyed taking you down the self-publishing path and, should you need me, I am but an email away.

Good Luck with your journey and remember; it's Your Book, Your Journey.

Daniella Blechner ☺

The Book Journey Mentor's™ Guide to Self-Publishing Workbook is designed to provide you with your personal space to jot down all the knowledge you learn along your book journey as well as record your personal responses to questions posed in *The Book Journey Mentor's™ Guide to Self-Publishing Handbook*.

Here at **Conscious Dreams Publishing,** we want the very best for you and your book. Although you will be well assisted along the way, we understand that, whilst the best way to learn is by doing, the best results are gained when we record our progress, refine our knowledge and create a clear plan on paper. It is also super useful for the next time you publish!

I hope this workbook serves you well and here's to a journey to remember!

Daniella Blechner at Conscious Dreams Publishing ©

ABOUT THE AUTHOR

Daniella Blechner is a UK-based award-winning entrepreneur, founder of Conscious Dreams Publishing, bestselling author and Book Journey Mentor™ who lives in South London. She is an avid author who is passionate about transforming diverse writers into successful published authors.

Over the last five years, she has published over 170 books and mentored over 200 authors and aspiring authors assisting them in transforming their powerful stories and messages into successful books.

Achievements include securing international press coverage for one of her young authors, Tiana, (7) author of *My Afro* on BBC, ITV, Channel 5, Good Morning America, Breakfast Television Canada and The Kelly Clarkson Show.

Other achievements include surviving lockdown alone, gaining 400+ comments on a post about what to do with cabbage during lockdown, completing the Don't Rush Challenge, living in Tanzania as a voluntary teacher whilst getting away with speaking broken Swahili and climbing to the top of Mt Kilimanjaro! She is the author of eight books and her debut book *Mr Wrong* became a bestseller beating Steve Harvey's *Think Like a Man, Act Like a Lady*.

Daniella won the 2007 Film Fund Award from Lewisham Film Initiative to complete her poetry based short drama *Hair We Are* for the Black History Month Short Film Challenge. The film won 3rd Best Film at the Images of Black Women Film Festival and has been screened at Chicago International Children's Film Festival, Pan African Film Festival, LA and BAMKids Film Festival in New York and was also screened on ITV Local. She was also shortlisted as a writer for Channel 4's Coming Up Initiative.

Daniella is also an English teacher with 15 years' teaching experience and has published authors from 7 years old to 84. She is looking for compelling stories and page-turning plots with unique and diverse characters as well nonfiction books with powerful messages. She is passionate about providing a platform for authors to have their voices heard and stories shared so that they can educate, inspire and empower for generations to come.

- www.consciousdreamspublishing.com
- www.consciousdreamsbookshop.com
- daniella@consciousdreamspublishing.com
- www.facebook.com/consciousdreamspublishing
- www.instagram.com/consciousdreamspublishing
- www.linkedin.com/in/daniellablechner

Acknowledgements and Thank Yous

Thank you to my typesetters Nadia Vitushynska and Oksana Kosovan who never fail to be consistent, efficient and professional.

Thank you to Jae Thompson AKA CVA Jae for the phenomenal cover design. Jae never disappoints and always works with the swiftness of a hawk. Professional and creative are his middle names!

Thank you to my editors Wendy Yorke and Anna Yorke.

Thank you to my entire Conscious Dreams team, who, without you, what I do would not be possible.

Last, but not least, thank you to you. Thank you for trusting in **Conscious Dreams Publishing** and in me as your Book Journey Mentor™. Publishing a book is a big step in anyone's life and I thank you for showing up and stepping up and investing in YOU!

Transforming diverse writers
into successful published authors

Let's connect

www.ingramcontent.com/pod-product-compliance
Lightning Source LLC
Chambersburg PA
CBHW050718090526

44588CB00014B/2332